GW00890442

HOW TO SPEAK
OASIS

LEARN TO TALK LIKE
A ROCKSTAR

Professor Mads Forrit

HarperNorth
Windmill Green
24 Mount Street
Manchester M2 3NX

A division of
HarperCollinsPublishers
1 London Bridge Street
London SE1 9GF

www.harpercollins.co.uk

HarperCollinsPublishers
Macken House
39/40 Mayor Street Upper
Dublin 1
D01 C9W8

First published by HarperNorth in 2024

13579108642

Professor Mads Forrit asserts the moral right
to be identified as the author of this work

A catalogue record for this book
is available from the British Library

HB ISBN: 978-0-00-875230-9

Printed and bound in the UK using 100% renewable
electricity at CPI Group (UK) Ltd, Croydon

If you're not in it to be bigger than the Beatles, it's just a hobby.

NOEL GALLAGHER

If I wasn't a musician I don't know. I'd be God, maybe? That would be a good job.

LIAM GALLAGHER

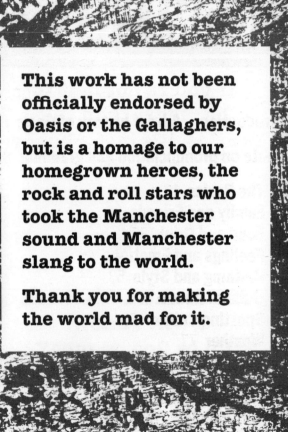

CONTENTS

Introduction – A brief history of Oasis 6

A note on pronunciation and grammar 8

1. **The Basics** 13
2. **Family and Friends** 25
3. **Food and Drink** 35
4. **Feelings and Emotions** 45
5. **Clothing and Style** 53
6. **Out and About** 61
7. **Sporting Culture** 69
8. **Weather** 77
9. **Noelism v Liamism** 83

Useful Poetic Idioms 94
Further Reading 100

A BRIEF HISTORY OF OASIS

Whether you want to be a rock and roll star, or you've recently remortgaged your house to be able to afford to go and watch some stars, unless you were born within sight of Manchester's giant Vimto bottle statue, you might need a little help decoding the language of the (rock) gods.

Oasis is a complex language with a rich and vibrant history. Its origins are thought to lie in the 1st century, where a fragment of the gospels has been translated as:

> **And God said: 'Let there be light.**
> **And lo, there was sun-shee-ine.'**

It is also, of course, via Egyptian, Greek and late Latin, where we derive the English word, *Oasis*, broadly understood to mean a fertile spot in an otherwise barren desert full of southern bed-wetting shite.

It can be found throughout the canon of English Literature, notably the 14th century epic, *Sir Gawayne and the Grene Knight*.

> **Where werre and wrake and wonder**
> **Bi syþez hatz wont þricke,**
> **And oft boþe blysse and blunder**
> **Fur our kid was beeing a righte dicke**

There are frequent references throughout the works of Shakespeare, especially the character of the fool in King Lear.

[Enter a Fool in a parka, with shoulders swinging]

Fool: Now then, now then, now then, For ton-i-ei-ight, might your rock roll to the stars, my nuncle?

And recent archival research has even uncovered an early draft of Rudyard Kipling's beloved poem 'If' that made powerful use of Oasis.

If you can fill the unforgiving time With each full day's worth of candle lit, Yours is the Earth and song and rhyme, And—which is more—you'll be f***ing mad for it!

But it is in the late 20th and early 21st century that Oasis has undergone a remarkable renaissance and has left its traditional heartland in the northwest of England to be spoken throughout the whole world. Even that London.

Building on the ground-breaking scholarship of Gallagher and Gallagher, what follows is the first definitive phrasebook for spoken Oasis. We hope you will find useful phrases for any occasion and that any Oasis speaker will, right here, right now, know what you mean.

A NOTE ON PRONUNCIATION AND GRAMMAR

As with many northern dialects,
H-dropping is common –
head becomes *'ed*.
Hello becomes *'ello*.
Vowels sounds have less distinction.
'**Strut**' and '**foot**' rhyme,
as do '**but**' and '**put**' and '**gas**' and
'**glass**'. Also – '**myself**' and '**no one
else**', '**tonic**' and '**want it**', '**laugh**'
and '**autograph**', '**BMW**' and '**Yellow
Submarine**'.

The emphasis of *g* after *n* is retained, noticeable in words like ***sinGer***, ***finGer*** or ***minGer***.

Oasis is unique in that it lengthens vowel sounds beyond what is standard in most other romance languages.
For example, '**need**' is '**neeeeeeeeeeeed**', '**believe**' is '**belieeeeeeeeeeeve**' and '**tonight**' is pronounced '**toni-e-i-e-i-e-ight**'.

In conversational Oasis, there is a habit of adding clauses to sentences where they may not seem strictly grammatically necessary to non-Mancunians/soft southerners. For example '**I'm hungry, me**' or '**what it is, right…**'

In addition, the use of '**and that**' as a non-specific additional clause, as in **'I'm going home to tidy up and that'** can be initially confusing to those who've not had the good fortune to enjoy an extended stay in the jewel of the north.

Certain phrases are compounded, so '**do you know what I mean?**' becomes '*knowworrimean?*' and '**yes I am very mad for it**' becomes '*fookinmadferrit*'.

The frequent habit of layering what can at first appear to be tautologies in reply to a question can wrongfoot the inexperienced.

'**How are you?**'

'**Yeah, sound, sorted, mental, madforit.**'

But don't worry. With a little practice you'll soon get the hang of it!

THE BASICS

CHAPTER 1.

When learning how to speak Oasis, Liam and Noel Gallagher are your best teachers. Follow their lead, and you'll not go far wrong. Included here is some of their most widely shared wisdom, at the start of each chapter along with a guide to lesser-known and local phrases. Adopt the classic Oasis-stance if you need when speaking.

> You're asking if I'm happy? I've got 87 million pounds in the bank, I've got a Rolls Royce, I've got three stalkers, I'm about to go on the board at Manchester City, I'm part of the greatest band in the world. Am I happy with that? No, I'm not! I want MORE!!

NOEL GALLAGHER

> I'm an average lad who was born in Burnage who played conkers. Conkers, mate. Conkers. The lot. And now I'm in a band and nothing's changed.

LIAM GALLAGHER

Hello

Now then?

A general all-purpose greeting that can be roughly translated as 'so, here we are, both of us briefly together in this precious flickering present, which can be found somewhere between now and then. How are you finding it?'

Ay up?

This is the informal, friendly version, to be used with younger family, friends and siblings.

Ow do?

This is the more formal greeting, used for acquaintances and older family members.

Alright?/you alright?/y'alright?

This greeting is rhetorical. Do not worry about replying with how you actually are, as this will horrify people. Simply replying y'alright will suffice.

Alright cock/cocker

This can wrongfoot those unprepared for it, but it is intended as an affectionate greeting.

Note: it is inadvisable to initiate this greeting with strangers.

Goodbye
Ta'ra (polite)
Do one (impolite)
F*** off (Liam)

Excuse me
Ee arr

Note: This can be used both to get someone's attention at the beginning of a sentence and when passing someone something, such as a rag pudding or butter pie.

Pardon me?
Yer wot?

Sorry
Soz

Something
Owt

Anything
Owt

Nothing
Nowt

Note: You don't get owt for nowt.

No
Nah/Nah man/Nah mate

I am very much looking forward to having a really nice time tonight
I'm mad for it/madferit/fookinmadferit

I would like you to reconsider that
Give your 'ead a wobble

Please mind your own business
Wind ya neck in

This is decent
Sound

This is reassuringly reliable
Sound as a pound

Whatever I say next, however rude and/or insulting, you are not allowed to be annoyed by it...

I'm not being funny like...

Note: It doesn't matter what you say – *you smell of otter faeces/your mum looks like the rotting corpse of a hippopotamus/ THAT is the single worst haircut I have ever seen* – this useful construction renders what follows entirely benign.

This is incomparably good
This is different gravy

Note: If you are complimenting someone's gravy, belt or top, it is probably better to use *this is mint*. If you are complimenting mint-flavoured gravy then you can use an alternative expression like *this mint-flavoured gravy is sound*. If you are complimenting a sound it is best to say *This is bangin'*, unless the excellent sound has been produced by banging, in which case you should say *That banging is different gravy*.

This is good
Mint

This is very good
Proper mint

This is extremely good
Sick

This is great
Bangin'
Beltin'
Top

Stop withholding financial support
Stop being tight

This is suboptimal
This is bobbins

This is horrible
Rank

This is unpleasant
This is grim

This is mean/fake
This is snide

This disgusts me
This is 'angin'
This is mingin'

This is the worst thing I can think of
Damon Albarn

Thank you
Ta/Cheers/Nice one/Top one (informal)
F*** off (Liam)

Very/extremely/really

Proper

Dead

Well

Note: If someone has definitely died then you should use the construction *proper dead*. If something is very proper, you should say it is *dead proper*. *Well dead* is acceptable, as is *well proper*, *dead well* and *proper well*. But nothing will single you out as a non-Oasis speaker more quickly than saying someone is *dead dead* or *well well*, or that something is *proper proper*.

FAMILY
AND
FRIENDS

CHAPTER 2.

Oasis is a language deeply rooted in family ties. It carries an especially rich collection of affectionate insults for male siblings, which Liam and Noel demonstrate best.

> **Sure Noel is good.
> But I'm better.**
>
> **LIAM GALLAGHER**

> **Liam only has two problems -
> everything he f***ing says and
> everything he f***ing does.**
>
> **NOEL GALLAGHER**

sibling insults

Very few Oasis speakers will manage the flair and lyricism of the Gallagher brothers. High-poets of Oasis, their rich levels of allusion and musicality set a high bar for Oasis learners.

'He's a man with a fork in a world of soup'
NOEL GALLAGHER

- You are a very angry man.

'I liked my mum, until she gave birth to Liam'
NOEL GALLAGHER

- I do not like you.

'Oi, tofu boy'
LIAM GALLAGHER

- You are soft, metropolitan and have lost touch with your authentic northern roots.

'Sit down. You've had too many G&Ts'
LIAM GALLAGHER

- You are talking nonsense .

'I love our kid, but not as much as I love Pot Noodles'
NOEL GALLAGHER

– I have my priorities correct in life.

I would scream 'somebody pass me the stepladder as I can't reach the cornflakes'
LIAM GALLAGHER

– You are short.

'I can play him like a slightly disused arcade game'
NOEL GALLAGHER

– I am a master of people skills/I was quite good at Pacman.

'I think it's unsophisticated music. For unsophisticated people. Made by an unsophisticated man'
NOEL GALLAGHER

– You are somewhat lacking in sophistication.

'You have a new song called Once, which is the exact amount of times it should be played'

NOEL GALLAGHER

– I do not think your new song is very good.

'Potato'

LIAM GALLAGHER

– Your head looks like a potato *or* your intellect is on a par with a tuber *or* you have the conversational skills of a complex carbohydrate.

useful family and friendship terms

What follows is a brief glossary of useful words and phrases relating to friends, family and relationships.

Bessies/Bezzies – best friend

....

Cock – a term of endearment. Often used as part of an enquiry as to your status 'y'alright, cock?'

Note: It's very important to get the order of words right as 'Your cock alright?' is almost always an inadvisable question.

....

Chuck – dear

....

Fella/Feller – man, especially boyfriend.

....

Flower/Petal – a term of endearment, similar to love or sweetheart.

Get – (believed to be related to the southern variant git): – an unpleasant/contemptible person.

He's not as green as he's cabbage looking – though his appearance may suggest he's stupid, he is in fact not as stupid as you might think he is.

Lass – girl

Nippers – children

Our kid – often pronounced 'are kid', it means a sibling but also a close family member or friend. A name can also be inserted as in 'Is our Noel coming?' or 'Has our Liam headbutted a unicorn again?'

Soft lad – unsound of mind and/or body.

FOOD AND DRINK

CHAPTER 3.

Whether you're the kind of person who only needs cigarettes and alcohol, makes a meal, only to throw it up on Sunday, or is caught trapped under a supernova of champagne, there is something for everyone in traditional Oasis food and drink culture, an arena which the Gallaghers have great knowledge.

> I love them.
> Particularly that point a few
> years ago when they said
> 'do you know what they don't
> actually give you cholesterol',
> I was like right, crack on with
> the f****** eggs then.

NOEL GALLAGHER

> What would be my last meal?
> An egg.

LIAM GALLAGHER

meal names

Though breakfast retains its traditional English meaning, other meals are named differently, so make sure you are up to speed.

Dinner – Lunch

Tea – Dinner/supper

A brew – Tea

Supper – A small bonus meal between dinner and going to sleep.

useful phrases

I'm gaggin' for a drink – I am thirsty.

I'm spitting feathers here – I am very thirsty.

My stomach thinks my throat's been cut – I really am very hungry.

You coming out for a couple of scoops?
– Would you like to join me for some alcoholic drinks?

Note: Confusingly, if you are ever invited for a 'quick one' by an Oasis speaker, this will not be one swift drink. Instead, you will almost certainly wake up 12 hours later in a bus shelter with kebab meat in your hair.

A-Z food names

Bangers – sausages

Bap/Barm/Barm Cake/ Breadcake/Bun/Cob/ Muffin/Roll/Tea Cake
Bread: much as the indigenous peoples of the North American arctic are said to have numerous words for different sorts of snow, Oasis speakers have a rich and nuanced terminology. But for bread.

Bury Black Pudding – a mix of pig's blood, onion, oats and spices held within the lining of animal stomach. Then eaten.

Butter Pie – confusingly this pie consists of pastry, onions and potato.

Butty – a sandwich of any sort.

Chippy – a fish and chip shop.

Chips and Gravy – a delicacy consisting of fried chipped potato but rather than being served with salt and vinegar, they are served with a rich gravy.

Chuddy – chewing gum.

Note: this is singular. A chuddy. Not *some* chuddy.

Corned Beef Hash – a dish made of tinned, salted beef, fried with onions and potatoes.

The Eccles Cake – a small round pie of flaky pastry filled with currants and topped with brown sugar. Also known as Dead Fly Pie.

Manchester Caviar – peas which are soaked overnight in water with baking soda before being cooked giving them the prized 'mushy' texture.

Manchester Tart – a baked shortcrust pastry tart spread with raspberry jam, custard, topped with coconut flakes and a maraschino cherry. Can also contain sliced bananas in custard. Proper posh.

Meat and Potato Pie – a pie with meat and potatoes in it.

Parched Peas – a delicacy consisting of purple podded peas. But rather than a rich gravy they are served with salt and vinegar.

Peas Wet – peas served with the water they were cooked in. Along with gravy these can be requested by asking for 'owt moist' at most chip shops.

Pop – a fizzy drink

Rag Pudding – minced meat and onions wrapped in a suet pastry cooked in a cheesecloth.

Scran – food

FEELINGS
AND
EMOTIONS

CHAPTER 4.

Oasis is an expressive, emotional language with a rich and nuanced vocabulary across all elements of human feeling, as Liam and Noel so richly demonstrate.

Not being loved and not being able to love. That's my biggest fear.

LIAM GALLAGHER

I like to think I keep it real. Liam keeps it surreal, and somewhere between the two we get on all right.

NOEL GALLAGHER

can't fight the feeling

Ave it! – an exclamation of celebration, usually after something has been successfully achieved, like a goal for your football team.

Bag on – in a mood.
'Has Liam got a bag on?'

Buzzin' – really very happy.

Chattin' Macca – talking nonsense.

Chufties – feeling happy or pleased.

Chufty badge – sarcastic fictional award.
'You managed to fetch yourself a glass of water. What do you want, a chufty badge?'

Cob – when someone has one on, it means they are angry. *'What's up with our Liam? He's got a right cob on.'*

Deck – to strike or punch, as in *'I am just about ready to deck you.'*

Getting on my tits – they are annoying me.

Give over – stop it, I don't believe you.

Is it ecker's like – I really do not agree with you.

Lamp – to hit someone as in *'if you deck me, I'll lamp you.'*

Mardy – moaning, or moody/surly.

Mither – hassle, trouble or bother.
'I can't be mithered to go to the big shop.'

Out of order – rather than meaning non-functional, this indicates behaviour that is not acceptable. This can be intensified by using the superlative: *Bang out of order.*

Pecking my head – you are annoying me.

Seeing your backside – beginning to be annoyed.

Shut yer cake 'ole – be quiet.

Skriking – loud crying or screaming.

Soft – silly

Strop

– a tantrum or sulk.
Can be used as a
noun and verb:
'Is Noel having a strop?'
*'Ah great, is our kid
stropping?'*
*'Are you throwing
a strop?'*

CLOTHING AND STYLE

CHAPTER 5.

Oasis culture has a distinctive and easily recognisable clothing style, which the Gallagher brothers showcase.

> **You know that thing they have in Switzerland, the Hadron Collider, where they're just smashing atoms into each other to see what the f**k happens? I think Liam's got one of those in his house which is just throwing desert boots at each other, in the hope that they will f**kin' create some kind of fusion, and out will pop the perfect desert boot that will never be bettered by any other human being.**

NOEL GALLAGHER

> **F**k them little sp*nkbubbles I've seen better dressed ROADIES.**

LIAM GALLAGHER

street style

Bells – fingers

....

Bins – spectacles
Not to be confused with 'top bins', which
is the top corner of the net in a football
goal and the best place to aim for.

....

Bog – toilet

....

Bonce – head

....

Napper – head

....

Closet – toilet

....

Duds – underpants

Couldn't stop a pig in a ginnel

– that person has bandy legs, such that, were a pig to run at them in an alleyway, the pig would be able to run through the gap in their bandy legs.

Could eat an apple through a letterbox
– they have big teeth.

Fit – attractive. Mainly of people, but can also be used in relation to an especially tasty pie.

Gigs – glasses

Kecks - trousers

Kippered - tired

Lothered - sweating

Newtons - Manchester rhyming slang: - Newton Heath, teeth.

Parka - essential outerwear

Pow - haircut

Salfords - Manchester rhyming slang. Salford Docks: - socks.

Smuv - a winter coat.

Your hair is full of lugs
– your hair has knots in.

**What did they cut
your hair with, a knife
and fork?**
– have you considered
changing barbers?

OUT AND ABOUT

CHAPTER 6.

A big part of Oasis culture is spending time with your friends, loved ones and people you bump into on a ferry. Greet them with the same level of affection Liam and Noel are known to show for people and places on their travels.

> **I am a tender, beautiful and loving guy that happens to slap a photographer now and then because they get in my way.**
>
> **LIAM GALLAGHER**

> **If I ever get to go to the moon, I'll probably just stand on the moon and go 'Hmmm, yeah…fair enough… gotta go home now.'**
>
> **NOEL GALLAGHER**

home and away

Absolute scenes
– an event of note.
'Last night, we went
to Greggs after the pub
and our kid ate four of
the jumbo sausage rolls.
Absolute scenes'.

Angin' – Crapulent

Ave it – get in/hooray. Especially useful if
throwing an empty can into a park bin.

Cadge a lift – to obtain passage in a friend's vehicle.

Dibble – the police. Alternatively: *Rozzer*.

Fettled – to repair, fix or mend. *'I'll have to get a taxi, my car is getting fettled.'*

Gaff – house

Get off and milk it – Hello there (to a cyclist).

Ginnel – an alleyway or walkway. *'I'm going to go for a slash in this ginnel.'*

Gotta chip, it's hair washing time – right, it's time for me to leave.

Lash – to get on the lash means to get drunk. Alternatively: to get on the razz.

Leg It/Peg It – to run quickly. Often used in conjunction with dibble/rozzer.

Manchestoh/Manny – Manchester

Mooch – the act of wondering about aimlessly, much like the French conception of the *Flaneur*.

Nesh – cold. This can be used both in relation to objects, the weather and people. *'Our kid has always been nesh.'*

Put big light on – turn on the main light.

Put wood int' 'ole' – please close that door.

Sat here like piffy on a rock
– I am waiting for my friends to arrive.

Scrotes
– unsavoury characters. Sometimes also know as *scallies*.

Up Town
– the nearest metropolitan area.

SPORTING CULTURE

CHAPTER 7.

An important aspect of Oasis culture is supporting the football team Manchester City and denigrating the football team Manchester United.

> **I hate them and cannot stand them, their ground or their manager. It's a hatred that steadily grows. I hate them more than yesterday.**
>
> NOEL GALLAGHER

> **City always come good at the end.**
>
> LIAM GALLAGHER

game on

If you find yourself without a light blue shirt and still want to indicate your affiliation, here are a selection of openers that will have you fitting in in no time.

A Manchester Utd fan was complaining that he'd left two tickets on his car dashboard that morning and someone had smashed his window and broken in.
'Oh no, did they take the tickets, chuck?'
'No, that's the worst thing – they left two bloody more.'

A policeman caught two men sneaking over the fence at Old Trafford.
'Get back in there and watch the game until it's finished.'

What do Manchester Utd fans use as contraceptives?
Their personalities.

How do you confuse a Manchester Utd fan?
Show them a map of the city of Manchester.

What's the difference between a Manchester Utd supporter and a bucket of cow manure?
The bucket.

What do get when you offer a Manchester Utd fan a penny for their thoughts?
Change.

What's the difference between passing a kidney stone and listening to a Manchester Utd fan talk about football?
One's an almost unbearably painful experience and the other one is passing a kidney stone.

Why do people take an instant dislike to Manchester Utd fans?
It saves time.

On a European trip to play a Romanian opponent, the Manchester Utd team visited an orphanage.
'It was heart-breaking to see their sad, joyless faces in which all hope had been extinguished,' said Alexandru, aged 5.

Why did the Manchester Utd fan miss his blood test?
Because he didn't think he'd revised enough.

A Manchester Utd fan was bragging in the pub about the fact it had only taken him 12 hours to finish a jigsaw:
'On the box it said 3-5 years!'

Did you hear about the Manchester Utd fan who spent 4 hours staring at the orange juice over breakfast because it had 'Orange concentrate' written on the carton?

Have you heard the one about the Manchester Utd fan who everybody loved?

No, me neither.

WEATHER

CHAPTER 8.

The Gallagher brothers have always understood that Manchester has a cultural and meteorological ecosystem of its own.

> **I am the most spiritual person in the world. I have feelings no-one else has.**
>
> **LIAM GALLAGHER**

> **The thing about Manchester is... it all comes from here.**
>
> **NOEL GALLAGHER**

singing in the rain

Oasis has a wide range of expressions to describe every sort of weather commonly found in the northwest of England.

As wet as a bastard – really raining quite heavily.

Autumn – A mellow, fruitful rainy season.

Beating it down – heavy rain.

Biblical out there – heavy rain.

Brightening up – it looks like it has almost stopped raining.

Bucketing down – heavy rain.

Drizzle – light rain.

Fine rain – the kind that gets you wet.

F**king it down – heavy rain.

Lashing it down – heavy rain.

Nice weather for ducks
– it is raining heavily outside.

P***ing it down – heavy rain.

Pouring down – heavy rain.

Raining cats and dogs – heavy rain.

Shower – short-lasting rain/less than 24 hours solid rain.

Spitting/spotting – light rain.

Spring – a warm rainy season.

Stair-rods – heavy rain.

Summer – a brief pause of two or three days between rainstorms.

Tipping it down – heavy rain.

Torrential – really very heavy rain.

Winter – a cold, wet season.

NOELISM
OR
LIAMISM

CHAPTER 9.

Historically, Oasis culture has been split between the two poles of Noelism and Liamism as shown. Two distinct personalities, both incredibly self aware.

> # I'm equal part genius,
> # equal part buffoon.
>
> **NOEL GALLAGHER**

> # I'm not an entertainer.
> # But I do entertain people.
>
> **LIAM GALLAGHER**

Noelism vs Liamism

By answering the following questions, you will work out which one you are more aligned with.

1. When it comes to turning up for a work presentation would you:

a) Arrive early so that you can make sure you are prepared, have rehearsed with the audio equipment and make sure there is time to tweak every detail of the presentation you may want to?

b) Drink seven cans of superstrength lager on the train, have an argument with a tree and then threaten to throw a chair at your boss because he's a f**cking k***head.

a ☐   b ☐

2. Which of these bands do you prefer?

a) The Smiths

b) The Stone Roses

a ☐　b ☐

3. What is more important in a song?

a) Craft, skill and a killer melody.

b) The lead singer's killer f**king attitude.

a ☐　b ☐

4. What are you more interested in?

a) The perfect guitar amp.

b) The perfect desert boot.

a ☐　b ☐

5. How many syllables does the English word 'tonight' have?

a) 2

b) 6

a [ ]   b [ ]

6. What would you rather spend your evening doing?

a) An early night with a book.

b) Getting thrown off a ferry in Amsterdam.

a [ ]   b [ ]

7. Which of these descriptions better suits your understanding of the phrase 'rock and roll'?

a) Music and songs.

b) It's about being yourself, doing what you want and not giving a f**k.

a [ ]   b [ ]

8. What do you feel more comfortable holding?

a) A guitar.

b) A tambourine.

a [ ]   b [ ]

9. Are you more?

a) Cat

b) Dog

a [ ]   b [ ]

10. Who is most at fault?

a) Cain

b) Abel

a [ ]   b [ ]

11. How many syllables does the English word Sunshine have?

a) 2

b) 3

a [ ]   b [ ]

12. What do you think about the vocal technique known as falsetto?

a) A beautiful and expressive way of hitting high notes.

b) Not for me, soft lad.

a ☐   b ☐

13. You are required at an important pitch meeting at work, but you do not want to do it, do you?

a) Go through with it anyway. It wouldn't be fair to your colleagues not to. After all, you're a team!

b) Pretend to be ill, then stand at the side-lines with a can of beer heckling their pitch.

a ☐   b ☐

Answers

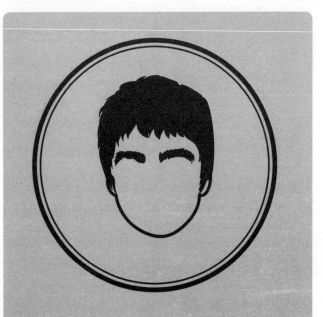

If you answered mainly a's, you are a follower of **Noelism**.

If you answered mainly
b's you are an advocate
of **Liamism**.

A BRIEF GLOSSARY OF USEFUL IDIOMS

Oasis contains a vast array of poetic idioms. Here are just a small selection of them as heard in the songs. Scholars have long argued over the meaning but some popular interpretations include:

Acquiesce
– an ambiguous, multi-layered word that contains elements of feeling alive, sleeping inside, seeing light that shines behind eyes, saying things that were unsaid, singing one's soul to sleep, as well as needing, believing and uncovering what's sleeping in one's soul.

Champagne Supernova
– unknown

Cigarettes and Alcohol
– something worth living for.

Electric

– the quality likened to being a woman who comes from an eccentric family, acting somewhat erratically whilst having a female sibling who one also likes but who has a blister on her hand; at the same time, they have a brother who you do not like, but who does have a mother with whom you share a somewhat mutual sexual attraction; in addition they both have roughly 12 cousins; though the woman is pregnant, you are not the father.

Half the World Away
– how it feels when you have a young body but an old mind and have been scratching around in a familiar hole.

Live Forever
– what you and I are going to do.

Morning Glory
– the place where, having been chained to a mirror with a razor blade, walking to a song you like on a sunny day and then finally waking up, you arrive. Or having an erection when you wake up.

Sunshine
– somewhere you could wait a lifetime waiting to spend time in, so you may as well take cocaine.

Supersonic
– the feeling of having had a gin and tonic.

The Eye of Your Mind
– a useful place to be slipped inside and potentially find a better place to play.

Waterfall
– somewhere your friend sits under where nobody can see him, or hear him call.

Wonderwall

– someone who, after walking many winding roads featuring blinding lights, but who you are still unable to say important things to, it now seems could possibly be the one who is going to save you.

SELECTED FURTHER READING AND LISTENING

All songs written by Noel Gallagher unless specified otherwise. Note: B-sides, deluxe editions, reissues and non-album tracks not listed here. Once you're a confident speaker of Oasis you can move on to these.

Definitely Maybe (1994)

1. Rock 'n' Roll Star
2. Shakermaker
3. Live Forever
4. Up in the Sky
5. Columbia
6. Supersonic
7. Bring It On Down
8. Cigarettes & Alcohol
9. Digsy's Dinner
10. Slide Away
11. Married with Children

(What's the Story) Morning Glory? (1995)

1. Hello
2. Roll with It
3. Wonderwall
4. Don't Look Back in Anger
5. Hey Now!
6. The Swamp Song (Excerpt 1)
7. Some Might Say
8. Cast No Shadow
9. She's Electric
10. Morning Glory
11. The Swamp Song (Excerpt 2)
12. Champagne Supernova

Be Here Now (1997)

1. D'You Know What I Mean?
2. My Big Mouth
3. Magic Pie
4. Stand by Me
5. I Hope, I Think, I Know
6. The Girl in the Dirty Shirt
7. Fade In-Out
8. Don't Go Away
9. Be Here Now
10. All Around the World
11. It's Gettin' Better (Man!!)
12. All Around the World (Reprise)

Standing on the Shoulder of Giants (2000)

1. F**kin' in the Bushes
2. Go Let It Out
3. Who Feels Love?
4. Put Yer Money Where Yer Mouth Is
5. Little James (Liam Gallagher)
6. Gas Panic!
7. Where Did It All Go Wrong?
8. Sunday Morning Call
9. I Can See a Liar
10. Roll It Over

Heathen Chemistry (2002)

1. The Hindu Times
2. Force of Nature
3. Hung in a Bad Place
   (Gem Archer)
4. Stop Crying Your Heart Out
5. Songbird (Liam Gallagher)
6. Little by Little
7. A Quick Peep (Andy Bell)
8. (Probably) All in the Mind
9. She Is Love
10. Born on a Different Cloud
    (Liam Gallagher)
11. Better Man
    (Liam Gallagher & Noel Gallagher)
12. The Cage

Don't Believe the Truth (2005)

1. Turn Up the Sun (Andy Bell)
2. Mucky Fingers
3. Lyla
4. Love Like a Bomb
   (Liam Gallagher, Gem Archer)
5. The Importance of Being Idle
6. The Meaning of Soul
   (Liam Gallagher)
7. Guess God Thinks I'm Abel
   (Liam Gallagher)
8. Part of the Queue
9. Keep the Dream Alive
   (Andy Bell)
10. A Bell Will Ring (Gem Archer)
11. Let There Be Love

Dig Out Your Soul (2008)

1. Bag It Up
2. The Turning
3. Waiting for the Rapture
4. The Shock of the Lightning
5. I'm Outta Time
   (Liam Gallagher)
6. (Get Off Your) High Horse Lady
7. Falling Down
8. To Be Where There's Life
   (Gem Archer)
9. Ain't Got Nothin'
10. The Nature of Reality
    (Andy Bell)
11. Soldier On (Liam Gallagher)

Different Gear, Still Speeding (2011) (Beady Eye)

(All tracks written by Gem Archer, Andy Bell, and Liam Gallagher)

1. Four Letter Word
2. Millionaire
3. The Roller
4. Beatles and Stones
5. Wind Up Dream
6. Bring the Light
7. For Anyone
8. Kill for a Dream
9. Standing on the Edge of the Noise
10. Wigwam
11. Three Ring Circus
12. The Beat Goes On
13. The Morning Son

Noel Gallagher's High Flying Birds (2011)

1. Everybody's on the Run
2. Dream On
3. If I Had a Gun...
4. The Death of You and Me
5. (I Wanna Live in a Dream in My) Record Machine
6. AKA... What a Life
7. Soldier Boys & Jesus Freaks
8. AKA... Broken Arrow
9. (Stranded On) The Wrong Beach
10. Stop the Clocks

BE (2013) (Beady Eye)

1. **Flick of the Finger** (Gem Archer, Andy Bell, Liam Gallagher).
2. **Soul Love** (Liam Gallagher)
3. **Face the Crowd** (Andy Bell)
4. **Second Bite of the Apple** (Gem Archer)
5. **Soon Come Tomorrow** (Andy Bell)
6. **Iz Rite** (Gem Archer)
7. **I'm Just Saying** (Andy Bell)
8. **Don't Brother Me** (Liam Gallagher)
9. **Shine a Light** (Liam Gallagher)
10. **Ballroom Figured** (Gem Archer)
11. **Start Anew** (Liam Gallagher)

Chasing Yesterday (2015)

(Noel Gallagher's High Flying Birds)

1. Riverman
2. In the Heat of the Moment
3. The Girl with X-Ray Eyes
4. Lock All the Doors
5. The Dying of the Light
6. The Right Stuff
7. While the Song Remains the Same
8. The Mexican
9. You Know We Can't Go Back
10. Ballad of the Mighty I

"The guns have fallen silent.
The stars have aligned.
The great wait is over.
Come see.
It will not be televised."

Sources and Attributions

Page 3: The Sunday Times 1996, The Sun 2005
Page 15: MTV 1996, Guardian 2002
Page 27: Addict, 1995, Q 2009
Page 28: Q 2009, Guardian 2019, Twitter 2020,
Page 29; X 2023, NME 1994, Spin 2005, Guardian 2019
Page 47: Daily Telegraph 2007, Twitter 2020
Page 55: NME 2015, X 2024
Page 63: Sky 2005, Twitter 2010
Page 71: Daily Star 2011, Manchester Evening News 2024
Page 79: BBC 1998, GQ 1998
Page 85: The Times 2001, NME 2007
Page 112: Statement confirming the reunion tour in 2025